The Four Moons

Rose Bowden

*To those who didn't laugh their socks off
when I said I was writing a book.*

Printed in the United Kingdom

First Printing, 2020

ISBN #: 978-1-9163850-0-9

This book is memoir. It reflects the author's present recollections of experiences over time. Some names and characteristics have been omitted/altered, some events have been compressed, and some dialogue has been recreated.

Cover photo courtesy of

www.sharontphotography.co.uk

Contents

Me

You will in some of this book detect an 'element' of exhaustion and desperation, well to be truthful the book is LACED with it but 'element' sounded much more positive.
Honestly, I am knackered, tired of the constant bills and lack of time in the saddle. I miss hacking out for hours on end and stopping at pubs. I miss making my horse pretty and sipping on a cuppa. I miss being sat next to people as smelly and as obsessed as me. I miss day long horse shows where I return home to a relaxing bath and a warm meal. These days, not only a husband and two kids - even the bloody dog pile into the bathroom to disturb my peace, or "keep me company" as they describe it.

I'm not overly sure why I am writing this book. I have no previous experience of writing anything more than a shopping list at home. Although work can get a little more serious but nothing to suggest I am particularly skilled in this craft. In fact if writing without spell check you would all be having a pretty interesting time fathoming my sentences.
So what made me decide to finally put pen to paper? Well, once a week I used to take my

daughter to a child's play centre. Whilst she enjoyed the various activities available to her, I decided to write a book. Where do you start? With your passion!

Oddly I would describe my relationship with all things horsey at the time as a little strained. If I remember correctly, my horse was on box rest and the whole process had me at a real low. In fact later in the book (*chapter 15*) I do discuss my thoughts on such matters, which explains a little more of my utter distain for box rest. I suppose writing helped me share a little insight into my personal experience giving me a sense of connection to those of you out there who are also battling to stay an equine Mum or Dad. The process of writing it all down in my notebook made me evaluate what was becoming a bit of a mystery to me. The mystery being, why was I so in need of owning a sodding horse when it was quite clear that early parenting did not suit my hobby at all?! To say the very least writing has been great therapy.

In addition to this I am a bit of a collector of old books, the kind you find in a jumble sale or in a house clearance. The type of book that has yellowed with age and has a few pictures in the centre to help you paint a picture of what the author is trying to share with you. All of my books have one thing in common....horses! I keep one of these books in my car or my handbag so that in times of boredom I do not grab my phone and start scrolling; instead I pick up a book. I hope that if you end up with this book in your possession, that you will chuck it in the cab of the horse lorry or leave it in the yard kitchen for when you have the time and the need to read a couple of paragraphs. Even if the book ends up yellowed and aged in years to come, I will not be offended as someone at some point will pick it up and have a read.

The book is also a little (very) self-indulgent. My aim is an easy read, for anyone with an equine interest or any hobby that deserves more time than you can give as a juggling parent. Not a self-help book at all, more of a confession to myself and to you about what is really going on behind the scenes of that amazing photo I just posted on social media. You know the one, that photo which displays me as a positive, successful, no nonsense parent, who never loses her shit, or throws her head in their hands wanting to scream various expletives. I do realise I am 'outing' myself here. Letting you all in on my dirty little secret.

Amongst friends and family I have a reputation of having a 'get on with it' kind of attitude. Ploughing on relentlessly, showing no signs of defeat or weakness. The truth in fact is that I am wading through fucking treacle on a good day and pissing in the wind on a bad day. However I deal with my downfalls and failures with the utmost humour and self-deprecating attitude (apparently). I can see no other way through it. I think if I was totally honest with myself, I would give up the whole shoddy, equine hobby set up, right this second.

We all have our coping strategies and suppressing my rage and disappointment is one of them; Nothing quite like a suppressed, English bird with a withering bank account, to compare yourself to. Compare away, if this book in any way gives you a giggle or at the very least put you in the 'kindred spirit' bracket then my work here is done. In fact if you do find some connection with my complete shit storm of a hobby and parenting life (parenting life, not such a shit storm, in fact I'm quite good at that bit) then we need to book a horse riding holiday together, when the kids are older. We can spend four guilt free days away, shit faced, riding our beloved steeds while getting lost via our ordnance survey maps. I have done this before and it's a great crack. Although you will have to hold the map, my horse will definitely throw seven shades of shit if I start flapping that about behind his neck!!

I did make the decision initially not to swear in this book, partly so as not to offend anyone. I begin to write using highbrow replacements for expletives but to be honest it didn't sound like me at all and I would have very quickly run out of words, even with a thesaurus. Don't get me wrong I do NOT make a habit of swearing, particularly in front of my children but I do work in a high stress environment. With day to day conversations containing many a colourful word, which I wholeheartedly find impactive and satisfying to say. Sometimes a swear word packs such a punch it gives the reader a true picture of one's feelings and experiences that no highbrow replacement can do. So I made the decision to not edit my experiences and not edit my feelings so apologies to you all. I have already apologised to my editor who due to some of the colourful language my manuscript was blocked by her firewall at work – awkward to say the least!

What my book also attempts to explain is that when you become a mum you are torn between caring for your new family and ensuring your horse obsession can still exist. Even if existence is not of its previous standard or anywhere sodding near. Don't be too judgmental and read on with humour and camaraderie. I want my cake and I want to eat it. It's all my own doing so as I say to many...........

'suck it up buttercup'- 'keep calm and kick on', or words to that effect.

Oh and I do suppose I need to add that my husband and I decided to buy a 'do up' Victorian town house to throw into what was already a pretty busy lifestyle. I feel you need to know this to have a true picture of the responsibilities we chose for ourselves. Carpet moth, rotten 70's porno bathroom and water pouring through the ceiling. We must have been high!!

I can confidently say that 2014 to 2016 was a fog of frantic DIY, nappies, shift work and horse shit!

1

The Addiction

The condition started many years ago. At the age
of 7, I climbed onto a horse while tagging along
at a friends sleepover party and Saturday morning
hobby. That was it. I was hooked. No way out! I
have even lunged my sister on occasion, so
desperate was I to have a pony.

Since that time I have been unable to switch off
the horsey part of my brain. You know, the one
where you look at a field while driving the car,
assessing its suitability for grazing or a bloody
good gallop! Don't even start me on golf courses.
Admit it we've all pictured ourselves belting
along a perfectly manicured course. In fact I can
quite believe some of you have done it, only to
explain to the green keeper that your horse
spooked and bolted!

When you break it down, the concept of riding a
horse sounds insane. A horse letting you get on
to its back. Crazy! It still amazes me now 38
years later, the fact that we can persuade a horse
to strap something to them (not a dildo for you
non horsey types reading this, I meant a saddle)
and then get on that thing we have just tightened

around their ribcage, its mind boggling. Of course in general I clear this from my mind while I am busy hunting or competing but whilst out on hacks the realisation creeps in and gives me a feeling of privilege. Admittedly the arrangement is driven by me as the human but there is enough partnership between me and the horse for us to coexist as one for a short while on any given day.

It's the same with travelling. I load my 16hh brut of a horse in to a relatively small metal container on wheels, taking him away from the area he was just in and unload him into any chosen environment and expect him to accept his surroundings and perform in some way.

I do try to avoid humanising my horse but he must regularly think WTF! If he did think like a human he would most likely need some kind of support group on social media. A group that could explain why humans get the horsey bug. Why we chose them and not bufallo or penguins to bond with. Why we then decided to not only ride them but then make up various obstacles for them and their human to tackle in a bid to win pretty ribbons. The group could also explain to them the reasons for why we chose them in particular. We have bred all shapes and sizes now, to accommodate our needs and wants. Fine horses, hairy horses, coloured horses, big, small, fast horses, plods, thankfully they do not think like us, they think like a horse which may be why we are drawn towards them in the first place.

The history of humans and horses is complex but very simple. The most useful, versatile animal available to us and we would not be where we are as a race without them. Nowadays it is a lot more complicated. I have no idea why my need and passion for them is so strong. Yes I can list their positive attributes and tell you how I feel about them but even now after all of these years I still could not really, in all honesty explain to anyone 'why horses'? We are a different breed; THAT I have figured out! Any other hobby that brings so many ups and downs while wiping out your bank account, should in theory become less popular. Yet with modern practices bogging us down, soaring livery bills, increasing costs such as vets and insurance being all part of the deal these days and we still continue to stride ahead.

As an adult rider I know I reflect a lot, which is probably why I take so long producing a horse and bonding with them. It's hard for me to expect a flight animal to comprehend what I am asking of them especially as I am over thinking it before they are. For this reason I have come to the conclusion that this is why I have found the whole 'mother who rides' a bit of a journey, a journey which at times, I have been very close to getting off. Thankfully my passion for owning my own horse always overrides the fear and exhaustion so those moments of frustration are usually followed by achievement and happiness and the addiction can be all consuming.

You will see from the front cover that I am as happy as a pig in shit when belting Benson (current and hopefully long term steed) across a stubble field. You may be looking at the picture and thinking, yes, that woman has got her shit together and she has balls.
I would agree, that is exactly how I feel in that picture, for those few hours - on that day - at the top of my game – a couple of years after childbirth.
Amazing, exhilarating, exciting, self-actualized! The best thing you can do on a Sunday with the most eclectic bunch of people gathered for a single purpose; to hunt the clean boot.

That day the four moons aligned and the photo for me records a great achievement and a great feeling. I am, in that photo, me. A mum who rocks with a great drive and passion to continue being a horsewoman!

I will discuss the four moons throughout this book. By the four moons I mean in order to achieve the most simple task while owning a horse you will need to get all four elements of your life aligned in order to get your arse in that saddle! I shit you not, it's tough. Some days it makes the G8 summit look like a coffee morning at the W.I. Childcare, horse, weather and you. Initially I thought the process would be quite simple but it's really not. When you break any situation down, there is a lot to organise, rely on and pray for. Believe me I pray to the equestrian lord many times a week!!! On occasion he answers and on occasion he throws every obstacle in my way. In fact he can be a real tosser!

TOP TIP - Prepare to fail, dust yourself off and wait for the four moons to align.

2

The Four Moons.

Moon 1 Childcare. Someone to look after your precious children. By this I don't mean just sit with them while you calmly ride your nag in the sand school (ménage). I'm talking about childfree, carefree time where you and your horse are left to each other's company without interruption or trips to the loo or snacks or shavings spiking a 4yr old foot in her welly, so badly she demands I stop exactly where I am and remove the giant shavings flake before she loses her shit or cries uncontrollably and makes me feel like the cruelest mother ever in the whole world – and breathe!

Moon 2 - The horse. Sound and ready to rock and roll. Good luck with that one.

Moon 3 - The weather. Not binning it down raining or winds so strong the weather people on TV have given it a name! Ice, fog, scorching mid-day sun will all hinder your plans for equine bliss.

Moon 4 - Us. The parents. Not lame, tired, wimpy or skint. Ready with a positive attitude and a seat to match or rival any Olympian.....ok I went too far, sorry!

So there you have it. Get that lot all ticked and you have yourself the perfect conditions for a fabulous horsey outing. You do know how rare it is for four moons to align don't you? Well, according to search websites it varies from rare to needing more luck than lucky heather and more patience than a Buddhist monk. However it does happen, (I am genuinely not sure how) and when it does, I am outta that door faster than shit off a shovel.

3

Juggling

Now I am prepared to tether my horse to the nearest solid object or let world war three commence among the other liveries if it means I get in the car for the school run, on time! You become your most resourceful when you become a mum, to the point where you will often seem very anti-social.

While at one yard for 6 months I only had one single rare cup of tea, normally riding and then dashing off to pick up whichever child I had 'loaned' to grandparents.

I do always try and make up for this flighty attitude by being friendly and always shouting "hello" and "goodbye", if you get a chat out if me, then well done. However, by chatting to me you have just made me that mum who has to abandon her car to the mercy of the traffic warden, run through the playground like a banshee and scoop up my waiting child, all while smelling of horse!

There is no doubt that I will have enjoyed chatting to you, I mean, who doesn't want to talk about horses!

Horsey mothers have less time and the knock on effect of an issue that is not itemised in the daily diary is glaringly obvious. Prior to kiddies I could spend an age sorting broken fencing, discussing poo picking rotas and whether there is any benefit in magnetic therapy rugs. I am just not that person any more. I just do not have the time. Organising days away, involving horse travel and activities has now become massively overrated and usually results in me realising at the very last minute that, maybe I am just trying too hard.

My week since 2009 has revolved around feeding times, naps (baby not me), cleaning, washing, shopping for food, work shift patterns, drop-offs and pick-ups, which on occasion has genuinely meant meeting my husband in some random car park somewhere, not for romantic rendezvous' but to swap the sleeping cherub to another car seat. I was never a napping mum, preferring to get chores done and ticking my daily 'to do' list. All sounds very organised but reflects in my permanent heroin chic look since 2009. In amongst all of this walking the dog, mucking out, and last but not least riding are all on my list!!!

I now have a whole two days a week to myself due to the arrival of school years. Initially thinking that in those 6 hours of 'me' time I am going to clean my house, walk the dog, food shop, chuck the car through the local wash, do some DIY on the house..... AND turn my horse into an Olympic prospect. It just never happens though but I get some of it done and have started to allow myself to slow down a bit.

Housework is no doubt, my least favourite; dusting to be exact. What a thankless job that is! A great Aunt (now passed) once said that "dusting was a waste of time as no-one ever notices if you do it or not". I am inclined to agree with her simply as she sways to suggesting I don't need to bother. I have even thought of letting the cobwebs build up so they can catch the dust. Well it seems to work at some of the yards I've been at.

I have in the past left all cleaning products out around the house and sprayed a bit of polish about to give the impression that I have been working so hard sprucing up the house when really I just gave up juggling that day and spent most of the 6 hours up the yard.

Then there's the tack cleaning. Never clean it. Not done one of those, take bridle apart and dip in a bucket of soapy water type cleans for years!! A quick wipe over with baby wipes does the job and even if that stubborn crusty bit of mud won't move then, so be it, it becomes part of the bridle.

So clearly my lack of enthusiasm for cleaning has even tipped over to my hobby. When I think about it, I do clean or have the responsibility of cleaning a lot of things. To think that one of my favourite classes at the local shows was 'tack and turnout'. Oh the shame! 20 year old me would judge 45 year old me, branding me a woman who has let myself go – and she'd be right.

As for mucking out, well the spirit level days are over! Bedding so straight you could see every right angle. Fluffy, cream coloured shavings, lovingly paid for and prepared so my nag can rest easy while in his stable. Now I'm satisfied if I remove most of the shit! Sometimes I even sprinkle a token few shavings on top to hide my shoddy standards.

I do still see those who spend a disproportionate amount of time on making horse beds all uniform and pristine. I would like to say I observe them with a little envy and nostalgia but to be brutally honest my only response is…what a waste of time.
The horse of course does not notice. He also does not give a donkey's dollop if he is not brushed prior to being ridden. In fact the horse will not give a shit about a shiny coat or a flowing tail. This is clearly proven by their immediate delight

in ruining any grooming standards, eagerly rolling in mud at the next available opportunity - usually 15 seconds after the head collar is taken off.

I am not saying that in previous years that I have not spent many an hour breathing in the yard atmosphere and spending hours debating what numnah I should next purchase or the importance of how many plaits will get me that red rosette. I have lived that life and loved it. For now, while a mum with young children, I am satisfied that my shortcomings will not break the horse and in fact have decreased my OCD levels of horsemanship which I think can only be good.

4

Savings

So 8 months pregnant, I waddled out of my lorry after a test drive from its new owner. In fact I recall sporting grey lycra leggings and a grey tent like wooly jumper. Realising that my impending maternity pay and partime working mum status was not going to make the yearly lorry plate bill, I decided to sell it. My faithful cattle lorry, which me and my dad had fixed up and added modifications, such as a fridge and porta loo. Also a secret isolation switch (my dad is a legend) so when parked up and abandoned on days out hunting, no one could steal it! Genius idea, thank you Dad! Years of freedom to come and go as I pleased were at an end but it had to go.

On the flip side the thought of not having to drive it through the yearly plate with grumpy sexist mechanics, speaking to me as if I had only just been given the vote, was a blessing. A lorry is great but due to the nature of a horse lorry's work load, they are notorious for being more of a money pit than the horse itself.

A trailer it was. I had the money from my lorry sale to buy a safe but old trailer. Well that was the plan until the bank of mum and dad stepped in and vastly improved my transport plans. Brand spanking, new trailer. My parents are legends and generous ones at that! They later stated that they were concerned that having children was going to dissolve my hobby and worried that I may give up. It was their way of making sure I was able to stay 'me'. For which I will be eternally grateful.

Oh and the equipment I then unpacked from the lorry! Why do we keep old bailer twine, old shoes, broken reins, mouldy, dry bits of leather incapable of being anywhere near useful?

Although I still find it hard to throwaway a mouldy bit of leather or a rotten head collar.

Memories creep in and remind me of which trusty steed wore that item and what fun we had. So now I have a box of mouldy old bits of leather and rotten head collars in the shed and I make no apologies for that. Cherished times.

Lowering your standards does force you to keep less junk. Your new purchases are less and completed with more thought. Less matchy, matchy and more; is it needed and practical? In general it is a slippery slope but downsizing and parenthood gets you back to the grass roots of it all leaving a few extra pennies. Well sometimes.

Top tip.........Fly spray – hundreds spent on exotic useless sprays which never last an hour, never mind a day! Like I have mentioned you rethink unnecessary purchases. Why spend £15 on some glorified perfume when old fashioned cleaning products do the trick. Watered down *Dettol* is cracking. Told you my standards have dropped! Please note I accept no liability for the use of such products on any horse, only my own! Oh and social media told me, so it must be true.

Savings have been few but I have learnt as I go. Letting out a little squeal of triumph (inside my head) when I decide against purchasing the latest rug or bridle. More recently I purchased a good 'old school' bit and it did not cost £150. My smug self has known for some years that the latest trendy bit will not make you a champion but it can be tempting to throw your bank account plans to the wolves and pick the more expensive.

5

Who's Who

My son (aged 9). A very non horsey boy, a planner who likes to know what is ahead, who is more careful than a health and safety rep. I will be putting his name forward for safety consultant at a future Olympic Games. He is very like me. A planner who likes to know what is ahead. Rarely throws caution to the wind and although has sat on a horse came to the realisation that they are a bloody danger and should be swapped for hobbies such as football or martial arts.

Now at the age of 9, I allow him to walk the whole 2 buildings away to empty the wheel barrow by himself. Yes, that's me, guilty, that type of mother. I have promised my husband that I will allow him to live a life of his own when he is 15. Maybe by then I will let him walk to school on his own, or at least covertly stalk him all the way. Disguising any sightings of me by taking the dog and pretending I am meeting a friend. Turning left or right at the next available opportunity in a very casual manner should he turn round. I am told by mothers of older children that this would expose my son to some serious issues both at school and in the future. Stalking for safety is too much apparently.

My daughter (aged 4 and a half) however is utterly fearless with a will to match. Most likely will be a competitor one day at the same Olympics! I suppose if they both do ever make it to the Olympics I will at least get free tickets. As for her walking to school on her own, well by that time I hope we can teleport. That way I can avoid stalking her, as she will no doubt subject me to many heart attacks while watching her negotiate traffic, playing 'chicken', as her and her equally fearless friends join in. Yes, teleporting sounds great.

I adore being a parent and it is without doubt the best decision I have ever made and I am pretty bloody good at it too. I am not one of those parents who had kids just to tick a box. I knew I would like my children and that meeting them and watching them grow would be every bit as fun as it was when I was their age. I have my parents to thank for that.

My husband, he will get his own paragraph shortly, titled The Reluctant. He needs his own paragraph.

Mum and Dad. My parents reply to my request for a pony was always...."When you're older". I think they lived in hope that the condition would go away. I wish it had, in its place would be manicured nails and regular facials, trip to the hairdresser to remove my grey roots. In fairness to them they we had a forces lifestyle so shipping half ton pet around the world was not a great or cheap plan.

As an adult my parents have been my enablers for want of a phrase. Constant support and in some cases have stopped me giving the whole thing up, reminding me that this is what I do and that it is a good thing and not the stressful money pit I sometimes refer to it as. My parents get it; they get the obsession and need. Neither of them horsey people but have embraced my hobby from the word go. Even to the point that I have now (at the age of 45) stopped mentioning if I have seen a new item of clothing or equipment that I need or like. For if I do their immediate reaction is to say "Oh we will get that for you baby girl". They deserve a great deal of recognition for their endless support in all things horsey. Dad for his engineering skills and his have ago attitude. Happy to muck in at any point despite his lack of horsey background.

Many years ago my dad broke his arm while trying to help me with my first horse. On reflection it was a bad match. I'd never ridden anything other than riding school horses and I chose a fresh 3 year old welsh cob as my first purchase. I can remember my father being bucked off in slow motion, landing on the floor and his arm taking the full impact. He got up and although clearly wanted to throw up with the pain, he managed to hold it together. Once home he then took a couple of pain killers and left it quite some time before seeking medical help, who confirmed a break. FUCKING NAILS my Dad!!!! We found him in the shed sawing off the plaster a few weeks later. Apparently the plaster was getting itchy and Irish blood heals your bones quicker.

As for my Mum. Not horsey at all and chooses her horsey friends wisely. She loves a big hairy type with a gentle nature. Mum is usually the one who can hear the truth behind my voice in relation to my current riding mojo.

My Mum does keep herself at a distance from the actual beasts and would never have any want to get on a horse. Not that I would want to witness such a disaster. I've seen my mum on a bike! After all she did once ride my old moped around our back garden and proceeded to catch her tracksuit on part of the fencing. My sister and I were totally paralyzed with laughter, as my mum could not let go of the accelerator handle, stretching her leisure wear at least 3 feet in length before it ripped. In the end the material gave up and mum finally came to a halt after we managed to spit out some words advising her to let go. Mum looked as if she had been ravaged by a pack of dogs. So I will assume that her avoidance of riding is a good thing. However she has followed me round many a year, soaking up the atmosphere at horse shows and a selection of yards.

My sister. All handbags and shoes. She did once have a pony years ago but saw the light and ditched the shitty wheelbarrows for days out shopping. Clever girl! However she is partial to the odd 3 day event location, providing her with endless shopping facilities and delicious snack breaks. I think it was Badminton in 1993 that turned her, swapping dungarees and cheesy crisps for fine clothes and bubbly. She now has two boys who will no doubt dampen her enthusiasm for shopping at Badders for at least another 5 years. The child fog is all powerful. Might suggest we revisit for my 50th celebrations.

The husband/partner. Usually 2 types.

The Reluctant.
Generally mutters the odd remark, ranging from "nice ride?" to "bloody horse". A deep dislike for all things horsey. Usually not helped by the distinct lack of pets while growing up; not even a goldfish. The Reluctant regards the whole thing as a smelly, expensive waste of time.

The Keen One.
Spend hours with you up the yard, getting involved but never riding. They smile lovingly at the affair you have with your neddy, without showing an ounce of jealousy. Probably the type to leave a gift wrapped name plaque for the stable door under the Christmas tree.

I am married to The Reluctant. Most definitely NOT the Keen One! In fact only the other day he had to come and find me to drop my daughter off at the yard. He came through the barn holding his breath and spitting out the rancid air as he reached the other side. During his ranting spit he claims that "we all must have something wrong with us to be able to hang out in such a pit of disgustingness". Moments like this for some reason stay in my memory and whenever I pluck them out, they give me a brimming smile which I am sure looks odd as I am going about my business.

And get this! He cannot fathom why after 38 years of riding, I still need private riding lessons on my own horse! Peasant!

One of the best reluctant husband moments was prior to children. Some years ago now The Reluctant thought he would make the effort to pop up the yard and see me and the nag (Darcy, next chapter). He drove his Mazda RX8 along the half mile pot holed track to the stables. I could see that the experience had caused him some distress, his precious sports car taking a hit each few metres as it meets the obligatory livery yard terrain. Despite his facial expressions he continued with his plans and walked with me in the dark to fetch the horse in.

Now to explain further, The Reluctant has never been and will never be rural. This incident occurred on a great livery yard with over 200 acres of land where horses were horses in large herds and able to roam for what now seems like miles, a rarity this far down south. More at home in the city and at the time did not even own a pair of wellies!! I know right, who does that??!! Anyway on this occasion he rocks up in his usual get up with various labels on. Hugo Boss being his favourite. The Reluctant tiptoes through the field and is ordered by me to wait near the gate. I carry on into the next field and as is usual, calling for Darcy. I stop and listen for a short time and realise that my call has resulted in the entire heard heading its way down towards me. Knowing horses as I do, I stand my ground, knowing that in general horses see well in the dark and will hopefully stop when they get to me. They did not, they all belted by, leaving me to turn round and follow them down.

Suddenly realising that The Reluctant was waiting near the gate on the inside of the field, I broke out into a cold sweat. The Reluctant would not know the front of a horse from the back and as I ran through the mud in my wellies (not easy) I pictured death looming. I shouted across "Move away from the gate". The Reluctant thought I had shouted to stay at the gate. Oh the panic, it was twofold. Should he be injured or killed, I will have lost The Reluctant and have to explain to his parents (now my in-laws) what a terrifying and messy end their much loved son had. Secondly if he did survive, this was not going to increase his interest or keenness for my hobby in any way!

Thankfully he survived. As I approached the bottom gate I could see reluctant frozen to the spot, facing away from me in a type of survival pose. Shit high in mud from heel to head. Hugo Boss trashed. I cannot repeat what he said as I think I swear enough in the book but all I will tell you is that his life did flash before him and he just asked to leave immediately. As we walked back to the car in silence I contemplated telling him about the rear view I had of him and that he may just want to pop it all in the wash when he gets home. I didn't say a word. I wimped out, I left him to discover that on his own when he got home. I cannot relay this story to anyone without being in fits of giggles as my humour fully embraces funny moments involving others misfortunes.

The Reluctant did get on a horse once, on our honeymoon and I have to say he owned it, cantering over the moorland in New Zealand. However, he explained it as the most terrifying thing he had ever done, even more than his student days bungee jumping!!!

Please do not feel sorry for me being married to The Reluctant. The Reluctant has numerous hobbies. Footy, golf, stag parties, marathons etc, giving me plenty of 'time in the book' for me and the "nag" as he calls it. In fact we now have quite a balanced attitude to it all. We don't discuss costs of anything anymore and after me losing my mind in the first early weeks of parenting, he realised that I may need some hobby time too. It has all worked out at least.

18 years into our relationship he did once remark on how dedicated I am to my hobby. Commenting that he has never seen me moan or tire of 'going up the yard'. He commended me on my dedication.

One of the nicest things he has said about my hobby. Well the only thing remotely positive.

Our dog.

ASBO, real name not disclosed to avoid potential legal suits.

Our current dog, chosen by The Reluctant and my son (neither of which have a great deal of input these days) due to her fluffy looks and well known good nature for family life. A boring brown cockapoo with the energy of a whirling catherine-wheel and the recall distance of at least a quarter mile. Like shit off a shovel and looks to break the land speed record when first let off the lead.

Previously I have had terrier types, just as unruly but usually happy to kill vermin or anything living within a fairly short distance from its owner. As for the ASBO, off she fucks. A brown dog disappearing into brown autumnal woodland does not make for a relaxed walk. She does however always come back which is a blessing but that's after she causes some disruption to other dog walkers in the far distance.

I once walked by a lady whose dog ASBO had just harassed. When I say harassed, she bounds towards a dog in the distance (at great speed) with an abundance of excited happiness and then once contact is made, heads for the hills yelping as if her leg has been torn off. Not pleasant for any party involved I assure you. I would imagine she acquired the skill whilst at the (unknown) puppy farm she came from; obviously prior to being moved to the cosy family home we viewed her at and bought her from.

The lady whose dog she had decided to go and meet showed me one of those coloured harness things which depict the dog's issues or personality or infirmity. Her dogs was yellow, which apparently means nervous. I do recall asking her if there was an ASBO colour. She seemed unamused.

What I will say is that the ASBO is now mine. Not only can she claim various ASBO awards, she has managed to impress me with her retrieving skills. I genuinely never knew dogs could bring stuff back. After all my years of owning terriers, who may as well have flipped me the bird when I even suggested they should consider bringing any toy back to me. A cockapoo will actually do stuff for you, who knew?!

ASBO has also adopted me. Realising that out of all of the humans available to her in our home, I am the best option. For those that know me, this is thin pickings. I have always been a dog lover and will always have one (or 2) in the home but they will not lead a king or queens life. No, love me love my dog signs here. No coloured harnesses for different moods. They get fed, walked and occasionally bathed. However I make up for my straight forward husbandry by letting the poor wretches off the leads!! They have a great time. Digging in the muck heap; belting across fields and through woods; days out with me in the horse lorry historically, now the trailer and truck. Not a bad deal and not a pooch parlour in sight after I stated to The Reluctant that ASBO would no longer being preened every 6 weeks for £40 and that I have a perfectly usable pair of horse clippers instead.

She has also improved over three years of her life and we can now take her to the local green (providing we keep an eye out for the more sinister looking dogs, who with no judgment would quite happily rip her from limb to limb for her odd ways).

So now my boring brown cockapoo is my muddy buddy. Mates for life; whether I like it or not.

So there you have it, an introduction to my crew. Now for the horses.......

6

The Horses

I have had the good fortune to have ridden or owned some cracking horses. I won't bore you with them all, just those since my introduction to parenthood. My mum always says I can spot a good horse. I think this is true but any good horse will give you a few bumps on the way, literally.

Darcy
Ten years of owning a warmblood ended abruptly. A kick in the field ended badly. A large vet bill. A damaged horse. Six month old baby and on maternity leave pay. Ask me if that was stressful! Don't tell me you've juggled parenting until you've moved a postage stamp square of electric fencing twice a day for weeks on end whilst keeping your 9 month old son safe and your warmblood enclosed within the flapping tangled tape. It was the stuff of nightmares. Despite this poor end our partnership was a great one. He was the most polite horse I have ever ridden. Maybe not so in the stable to yard staff but a true gent to ride who was built and bred for the arena but gave his heart to the hunting field. A stunning coloured lanky beast with a delicate

nose showing a little Arab in his blood line. He despised anything associated with the equestrian disciplines and came to me very sour and probably over schooled. He had been advertised as a show jumper but apparently would not jump a pole on the floor for any perspective buyer. Luckily for me, a friend who was also a vet text me one day after me mentioning the above horse, a green, sour 5 year old warmblood was not what I had in mind but I tried him and oddly trusted him from day 1. I did try for some years to get him to show interest in the disciplines but he was hell bent on regularly freezing on the spot at many a competition (mainly jumping) and refusing to move an inch. Never rude or visibly defying me, just frozen, not even an eyelash moved. He won, we hunted.

Eddie
A stop gap who gave me the confidence to take on my current horse. Again another coloured. At the age of 3 he was a little cracker with a big character. I bought from a show producer and good friend. If he were human he would be in a boy band. At the time I was very sad to lose him but he was co-owned and the partnership had gone sour so with hormones high and a 6 week old baby I sold my half. However as I have mentioned, bringing him on gave me (the nervous

type) the experience to know I could do it again and on a more challenging animal. Looking back he would not have been big enough but he was just the most straight forward fun ride.

Benson

A brut of a horse who just kept growing. I bought him when my second baby was just 8 weeks old (fucking madness). One of the most quirky horses I have ever allowed myself to get on. As a youngster has ditched me without thought and has endless stamina. He was bought from a local country chap who advised never to feed any of his horses out of a bag, a rule which I stand by today but only after realising feeding Benson pony nuts is like supplying him with cocaine. In all it has taken me 4 years to get this cracking horse to a reasonable standard. I hope this partnership continues until we are both old and grey. A close coupled chap with a large white blaze covering most of his face, giving him one of those eyes which shows a little white. A beard from chin to neck to belly when I first purchased him but once trimmed he transformed into a lush looking beast with a soul to match. He gives the best feeling when ridden. You know that strong forward ride that feels just on the edge of wired. As for elevation, he may be a cob cross but he has presence and a trot so active that my birthing, ageing hips will no doubt give up should we ever reach sitting trot levels in dressage. One of the friendliest horses and despite his average breeding, I feel the most talented.

One thing I have learned you can never repeat the same experience with a different horse. Each horse finds its own strengths and likes. What I had with Darcy was excellent and once we had established that all things competition was a no go, then we had more fun.
I have seen many people with or without children try to emulate their last partnership but I have yet to see it work. If you are the type of owner I am, where your horse is your only horse and you don't view the animal as a commodity, or having a specific purpose such as show jumper or eventer in mind, you tend to go with the flow.
I have neither the skill nor bravery to insist on my horse's CV before its ever even been sat on. I tend to go with what the horse naturally turns to. In addition to this, no matter how hard you try, your years prior to children will be impossible to replicate. Well unless you have a live in nanny or your own yard with stable staff. I have neither, nor a cleaner or a person to do my ironing etc etc.

I have wasted a lot of time, effort and energy, continuously failing. Instead I should have accepted my constraints and lowered the bar slightly. Benson, I hope I will have until his and my retirement. By then my children will be well on the road to their own goals, leaving me with plenty of time and energy to brush him to within an inch of his life!

7

Hunting

Oh and before all you antis start, I hunt the clean boot!!! If you're not sure what that is then you shouldn't be an anti! You are only part way in educating yourself about country pursuits. Oh and to add, I have never fox hunted and was vegetarian for 12 years. Just in case you were about to burn this book before reading another word. A little defensive I know but more recently the practice of any country pursuit has been widely commented on in social media and without going in to much detail here I just wanted to clarify my involvement.

Today I travelled to the opening meet, driving down the narrow lanes, assessing my confidence, or the lack of it! Listening to Peter Gabriel *'Solsbury Hill'* as my chosen inspirational music, while a 4 year old Benson bashed around in the trailer each time we stopped at traffic lights. It's a skill timing traffic lights to change to green as you approach them, believe me! However my nerves were getting the better of me so I swapped my musical inspiration for The Prodigy *'Firestarter'* in a feeble bid to switch fear into bravery.

What the hell was I doing taking a green 4 year old horse and purposely galloping it around the countryside? Shitting my pants AND full of utter desperate excitement is the only true description I can give.

I will also admit that now as parent I feel so responsible for my own safety and survival. I will always allow negative thoughts to pop in to my head at these times. What if I die today? Madness you may think and I would be inclined to agree but it is so true for me. I do struggle with the rational and the bat shit crazy at times of pondering thought. I mean reasonably, I should consider the possible consequences of what I am about to do. Hunting is rife with available mishaps and danger. A portion of that reality is part of the buzz I suppose and I did feel quite guilty buggering off for the day to potentially not come back. All sounds very dramatic but I did tell you this book would be a confessional for me and becoming a parent brings a whole other dimension to how I view my life. That and also imagining the words "I told you so" from The Reluctant, when he is told the news his horse mad wife has managed to wrap herself around a tree while out hunting.

Topped up with some heavy swigs of generously donated port while frantically changing into my boots and jacket in the trailer, praying Benson would remain tied to the ring on the side and not fucking off before I even had a chance to get on him! Off we went! Our first attempt to get back to where I feel I belong.

I will also add that this was only the third time I had cantered him properly. Too wimpy to canter him in the school, I had only completed a few strides whilst out on a hack with a friend who had kindly offered to be the lead, knowing that a young horse's first canter can go 'tits up' very quickly.

No, this is not the normal process and I really cannot fathom out why as a rider I find it an easier process to gallop across miles of land, yet a 20 metre circle fills me with nerves. Maybe it's the controlled element. I suppose a horse will naturally want to follow a herd of cantering horses but to ask him to circle the school as per my instruction seems more of an ask. Miles and miles of stubble seemed a good option. Yep desperate!

For this first hunt we both mainly shat ourselves. Apologies for the language but both he and I

would have used many a swear word during the morning had we not both been blowing out of our arses! In fact at one point I genuinely thought I was having some type of asthma attack until I remember that I was wearing a body protector that was clearly fixed too tight and my current fitness levels were that of a mum struggling through the local soft play centre obstacles.
I can remember seeing our hunt photographer as we belted from one field into another. I think she asked me if I was ok. I would imagine I looked a little pale and could not answer as my throat was now so dry, I had to stop myself from reaching and gagging.

Sadly I had been so keen to just get out there that day that the lack of preparation meant my hip flask, which was also abandoned during pregnancy a couple of seasons ago and left in my kitchen since the last time I had hunted, had fused shut with the remains of the last hunts port inside. Nothing to wet the whistle! Success can sometimes be very uncomfortable.

In all, that day he was a very good chap and I drove home grinning from ear to ear at the truly miraculous event that we had just pulled off. Damn it felt good.

For anyone with children knows there is a shit load of juggling required to get out of the house and purchase milk, let alone get a horse trained (ish), loaded, tacked up and survive a days hunting.

Benson has hunted since but in all honesty I am simply a passenger now. He locks on to the field master and that is where his goal stays for the few hours we are out. His record is pretty good and he is quite sensible but as the seasons have gone by he has become very confident so we have stepped back from hunting and redirected to dressage. This is my bid to keep him a woman's horse, which I WILL achieve. My god, I am being so polite....who am I kidding.......he is a train, a machine, a fucking beast but my god he is lush!

Our last hunting day together ended in disaster. He binned me after I threw caution to the wind and let him jump a jump that I thought was too big. I remember saying in my head "FUCK IT". This is rare for me as I am not really a "FUCK IT" type of person, much preferring a rational, practical approach. Mainly due to reflecting on the few times I have in my life that I have adopted the "FUCK IT" approach, it has all gone to rat shit!

By the time we had faffed about deciding we ended up bunny hopping it then he bucked twice due to me landing unbalanced. Undeterred I kicked on while he bucked, only for him to drop his shoulder (a favourite move of his), bin me out the side door then piss off with the field.

I did get back on after getting my wind back, helped up by two very lovely ladies which I think I forgot to thank. Looking back I was a little concussed and had to be reminded later about who peeled me off the floor. Short while later another kind member of the field on a very sane horse brought Benson back to me. Once back on, Benson then forced me over the next jump with all four legs in gazelle position. I have a picture to prove this, otherwise it's very hard to imagine and I did think impossible. He then proceeded to take hold of the bit and got quite unruly. By unruly I mean bolt!

I waited for my moment and dismounted, dragging him all the way back to the trailer park while he threw the biggest tantrum at my decision to stop his fun. To add insult to injury he then freaked out mid un-tacking and galloped up and down the enclosed field, with my very expensive WOW saddle dangling round his neck by a single hook from his breastplate. BASTARD!

One person in the lorry park suggested I hunter trial him. I'm not sure that was positive or negative comment. It was difficult to decide as Benson ploughed up the ground of a very posh, wedding venue type country estate.

Benson has the stamina of a long distance runner and the strength of a draught horse. That day I compiled an advert in my head, an advert that would start with the words, FOR SALE. Then I came to my senses and realised he was, at that moment, unsellable. Who on earth would buy him? Girthy to saddle. Shit to load. A lunatic on anything other than chaff. By-yearly mysterious illnesses halting any true progression in his competitive career. I couldn't give him away!

I look back at that day and reflect, accepting that Benson is a fantastic horse and one of the best I have ridden. However on that day I was done again. All the positive milestones had gone from my memory, blanked out by my idiot horse who today had crushed my mojo to the point of almost no return.

More recently a young chap has taken him out and had a great day but did feedback that Benson was very strong and that I was being too kind giving two reins on the cheltenham gag and that I should only bother with the bottom rein.

I wouldn't mind but I purposely kept him unfit so the young chap at least had a chance.

I will hunt again this year but only at training meets and with plenty of open stubble.

2020 update…..Dressage it is!!!!

8

Jumping Lesson.

Pouring, torrential rain. I receive a text from my instructor who is also confirming that it's pouring where she is too.

I, at the time, stood under a tree with my horse, both of us dripping wet, sheltering from the biblical downpour, waiting for a break in the rain to make a mad dash to the stable so I can tack him up.

I acknowledge her reasonable statement and suggestion to book another day like any normal person. However, I reply confirming that I can see in the distance, a small patch of blue sky and predict that the very patch will move on over our way giving us a mini climate and the feasibility of a lesson.

After all, childcare is booked, horse is sound, I have had some sleep and have a pulse. The four moons have aligned, well at least 3. The lesson must go ahead. It did and it was great, even the blue patch of sky hovered over us. Had it not I may have spiraled in to a dark place and shoved great amounts of chocolate down my throat for at least 24 hours.

On reflection I have assessed my desperation and observed myself from an outside point of view, seeing quite a sad individual who regards success as a list of ticked horse training goals. Prepared to stand under a tree while the weather pisses down, still determined and hell bent on a bloody jumping lesson. Honestly, quite sad.

A not so successful occasion was when I had a whole month to sort childcare! A month I tell you, a whole month!

Yep you guessed it, I cancelled the lesson, last minute due to lack of childcare.

Now this was no fault but my own. I simply get far too excited about my hobby and my enthusiasm to learn and improve my relationship with Benson overrides any rationale. That feeling of an impending lesson or day out hunting, even a visit to the tack shop fills me with excitement. I know for a fact that anything booked after the school run or into the evening is at risk of never happening. The 4 moons need to align and one of those moons being childcare, relies on The Reluctant finishing work on time. He didn't.

I have pictured my two lovely children sitting in the gallery while I bond with Benson. Yeah right. I can't even lunge Benson without someone needing a wee or poo. In any case Bensons not the most forgiving of creatures so I want to avoid jumping the dizzy heights of 2' (70cm for you young uns) and ending up being whisked off in an ambulance, leaving my two children traumatised and waiting for their dad who is already poised for the day he can genuinely and with good reason tell me I need to sell up this insane hobby.

Being so eager to achieve can get you into trouble! Being so desperate to reach that goal; fighting every inch of the way to ignore the self-doubt, fear and common sense. (I'll add a dodgy nerve tummy to that too), only to realise that I should have left it for another day.

Caution in some ways has become my enemy too. Overthinking. Having never been a brave rider, as a mum, I am now even more cautious. My drive has to override my fear. I get round this by accepting that things will just take longer. What most achieve in a couple of years, I have taken double the time and longer.

On a more positive note I have managed to align the 4 moons and am quite deserved of the title 'superhero' on many occasions.
Leaving the arena feeling like I have just been signed up for the British team! The thing is; it just

doesn't get old. The sense of achievement and buzz gets you right in the gut and flutters the heart.

9

Giving Up

Don't make the mistake of thinking that I have clearly lost my way. I have thought about giving up and also tried it. Sadly Darcy had to be put to sleep a short while after my first child was born so I did give myself a chance to be a normal person. I thought my detox was going well until The Reluctant confirmed that I was horrible to live with and that I should get another one. Bet he regrets that!

During that time I don't recall saving any money either. Instead the empowered feeling of having a chunk of disposable money available to me sends me off my tits with excitement. That's when I will quickly throw this money at facials, new clothes, eating out and whatever else takes my fancy.
These times have been short lived and just as well for there is no doubt that whatever money I would have sitting in the bank waiting to be spent on a new nag, would easily disappear if I ever left it more than a few months.

I do have peaks and troughs. Sometimes I really do consider packing it all up and releasing some serious cash on a monthly basis. Cash I can spend on shoes maybe, or replacing my ridiculously dated wardrobe. Problem is, that whiff just gets to you and you're powerless.

Those occasional moments of equine brilliance really do keep you hooked. The mud, cold, injuries, cost and juggling will all do their utmost to put you off. That single moment of utter satisfaction in the saddle cancels it all out. I only have to sit on Benson in the school and have him push on into trot to feel like a top dressage diva. I get back into my car after my couple of hours at the yard and all is well. I feel accomplished and settled. There is no doubt that it is a type of therapy for me. Exercising amongst nature. Alleviating the stresses of the modern world. Ridding the body of tense feelings and adrenaline. I could go on.

So you see, for me, giving up is not an option.

10

The Whiff.

You know exactly what I'm talking about. We fill our lungs when we get near anything equine. Even a tack shop can give you a hit, the unmistakable smell of brand new English leather. Rows and rows of bridles and saddles; pumping out a glorious leathery smell.

Burying your face into your horse's neck and inhaling. Just gorgeous! Although I would mention the jury is still out on stable ammonia whiff. That is rough!

My daughter greets me at the door. "Mummy have you been to Bensons? You are stinky!" Clearly I'm not making good smell memories for my children.

The whiff of a horse transports me to a place of calm and in my case childhood. Times when climbing trees and mud pies existed. Riding at the local riding school on a Saturday morning. Hanging around after to help with anything remotely linked to a pony; with no real concept of the reality of owning a horse.

I am a bit of a whiffer it seems. I do drift off into the world of memories when I smell the smoke of a coal fire coming out of a chimney or walk by a privet hedge. Those types of smell that take you back in a nano second, to a time and a place you store in your brain somewhere. Memories come flooding back giving you that great nostalgic feeling which wells up and makes you sniff stronger and close your eyes. Old second hand furniture and books get me too.

My most embarrassing habit is whiffing my kids. Yes, you read correctly, I whiff my kids!
I know we all love the baby smell, that's a given but I have a clear need to whiff my kids daily. I am even such a bad whiffer that my children tell me off. I have been known to flare a nostril when they are sat next to me watching TV, or (cannot believe I am writing this) at my worst when they are settling in to bed, snuggled in their blankets, all sleepy and cosy. That way I get a good whiff without any objections.
Writing this out is making me reflect on my whiff issue and yes it does sound odd. My sister cannot fathom it and slightly reaches when I tell her that toddler breath is divine.
I guess I am just a whiffer. So if it is horse whiff, cherub whiff or even privet hedges whiff, I am made in such a way that it transforms into calm nostalgic feelings and memories.

11

Pregnancy

On a serious note, pregnancy can be overwhelming and a little scary. Most mums will have quiet thoughts and anxiety about the unknown. Bombarded with help and information and making the decision on which bit you take on board and which you leave in the leaflet. Oddly one of mine was allergies, not the traditional food type allergy. What if my child were to have a serious or even minor, allergic reaction to horses? I am not alone in this. Only the other day while skipping the stable out, another new mum was chatting about her anxiety over the same issue. Her mentioning this made so much sense to me. I mean please don't get me wrong (or her), had this been the case then it would have been a clear decision in that the horse hobby would have to be put on the shelf for a long spell.

Isn't it odd how we can think alike? So strong is the need to have a horse or at least be around them, that we have to consider the consequences of one of our favourite things turning into a 'no go'.

I recently read a post on social media where a soon to be mum was asking for ideas on maternity wear for horse riders and if it existed. Well yes it does. It's called menswear. Mens t-shirts and jogging bottoms usually do the trick. Although I'm not sure that was the look she was hoping for. Well, I suppose the alternative could have been my early pregnancy look. Open zipped jods with a hairband holding in my dignity. Dignity, who am I kidding?! After childbirth dignity is non-existent. Half of Hampshire has had a look at my under carriage, or so it seems. Childbirth exposes you to a whole world of medical practitioners who for one reason or another need to check out your bits and bobs on at least a weekly basis.

My experience of riding whilst pregnant involved airline sick bags, the need of a small winch to get on and off or the use of someone else's body for 9 months.
I ballooned, ached and puked to within in an inch of my sanity. No small 'Mary King' bump for me. No demur occasional nausea for me. No, for me it was a full 9 month onslaught of symptoms, leaving me with a huge sense of relief when my little people arrived.

When they do arrive, WOW, you thought you loved your horse???!!!! Wait for these feelings! A lightning bolt of utter worship and adoration!

A lovely feeling, which at first, can be a little overwhelming. I have to say I was so steeped in maternal instinct that I quickly decided that I could never get on a horse again, or drive a car, or go back to work. Thankfully over time all of the previous were achieved as the hormones slowly left my body. Glad they did as that would have been a little full on for the rest of my life!

Then there's the *getting back on* issue. A fresh rested horse and a knackered human do not make for a quick return to the saddle.
It was an achievement to lift a bale without weeing my pants a bit, let alone haul myself back up the side of a horse and place my bum in the saddle. I envied anyone blessed with a pregnancy body with the ability to carry and give birth, with only a few days out of the saddle. You girls are out there and power to you. In fact I know a couple of you and frankly you are lucky I still speak to you.

Commiserations to those who follow my pregnancy path! It's gonna be a long run!

TOP TIP – keep your pregnancy pants. They make great giant comfy riding pants.

I love mine but I do hide away when changing into them as The Reluctant saw me once while changing and I think he nearly threw up in his own mouth. I suppose using them outside the excuse of weight gain and pregnancy was a bit of push and I will admit, more than a little unsightly. A hacking friend of mine, 10 years my senior was quite taken aback when I described my now baggy, skin coloured, apple catchers, informing me of her maturing years and that even she at her age would make more of an effort. I was going to leave this paragraph right here but prepare for some oversharing! When hacking now I sport a pair of sport cycling pants and a splosh of petroleum jelly to protect my foo foo and derriere from the ravages of pommel rub and cantle crush. I know right but for any woman who has endured childbirth will be more than aware; undercarriage is rarely the same after. Well that or I am in denial about my pre-baby 16inch saddle and need to buy something a little more roomy. Told you I was oversharing. Nah! In fact I recently discovered that chuff chaffing is a real problem, so much so that you can now purchase specific lubricants designed to apply to your bits and bobs which will not only render them chaff proof but it also gives them a whiff of lavender while you ride your steed around the country lanes.

Once in the saddle I did give myself goals. Well sort of deadlines, various milestones to achieve before getting back on.

Long lining for instance, I've done hours of it and loved it. Gets rid of the wobbly bits quicker than riding and increases the owner/horse bond, which may be a little rusty. Most of all it just gets you out there!

I'm not going to lie, I have considered strapping baby to my back and pounding the countryside whilst long lining. However my rational thought kicked in and I remembered I had a youngster at the time and seem to be a shit magnet, the idea was in fact ridiculous.

If any of you have done this, after considering the safety issues, then power to you. That's some hardcore horsey obsession you have there.

These cute little bundles arrive and can be all consuming. A while by yourself with your nag will make you a better mum and partner. Getting out there can mean anything, a hack, schooling, a show even. You'll get to see so other horsey obsessed people and will return home with a fresh vigor for nappies, bottles and housework.

Oh and don't worry too much about standards. I have entered competitions without a drop of water hitting my horse's body. We rocked up in hunting gear and un-plaited to dressage.

My attitude is, I've paid the fee and aligned the four moons, Cinderella will go to the ball. Disrespectful possibly, but the truth is, this is the best I can do today.

I read a quote once, something along the lines of *'stop brushing the horse and ride the horse'*. The idea came from a very capable cowboy on one of those social media pages. The quote gave me permission to lower some of my standards and just get it done.

Anyway our first dressage competition was fantastic. Highest mark ever but I forgot to salute. I was so excited that Benson had not binned me during the test and that I had remembered where to go, that I forgot all formalities.

Does it matter? No not really. Not in the grand scheme of things. I didn't have time to chat with the judge to explain our lack of etiquette or informal outfit. No opportunity to educate them on the various downsides to our dressage display. I didn't really waste more than a moment worrying about it. I was just so bloody chuffed to be out there again!

I promised myself that I would make a better effort next time and I did.

12

Standards.

Aim low people and you will never experience disappointment!

This thought process has helped me many a time. It takes the pressure off immediately. Us horsey lot can be programmed to get it all right first time and expect success. I have seen so many riders and owners putting too much pressure on themselves, making the whole experience a stressful nightmare. Some not even entering a competition as they fear they will not be in the top ribbons or their stable neighbour may beat them in the rankings. You never know how successful you will be and in any case your only completion at this stage of the game should be, yourself!

This is twofold when you're juggling between parenthood and your hobby. In my experience, 'have a go' attitude rocks. If the four moons are in alignment!

Not sure if its motherhood or my growing mature years but my standards HAVE dropped AND I secretly like it!

Cares are less too and as for drama, well that takes a back seat. I have worried in the past about the most ridiculous things, opinions of others with only their own interest at heart. Days and weeks consumed with the latest yard drama. Receiving unwanted feedback about my own horse husbandry. Anything like that would become so important to me that I wasted time and energy on the effects of such matters that I sometimes forgot to enjoy my horse. In fact I think we have all been at the receiving end of such unnecessary drama. Let's be honest it really is a load of old tosh at the end of the day. Today I am very sure of what it important and what my priorities are.

1. Does he have 4 sound legs?
2. Is he breathing?
3. Are we both content?

A lovely lady called Jane once said to me…."They are horses at the end of the day and they have a job". This is so true. I think we have lost sight of that in more recent years. Well here I am people, bringing you back to basics!

13

The Horse World.

Warning!! Please accept that I will take the piss out of myself as well as the various disciplines. My aim is not to offend; just give a light hearted reflection on what a mad bunch we all are and how my view has changed now that I have much less time.

Showing

Now let's make this clear. I spend a disproportionate amount of time looking a bit bedraggled. Kids, dog, horse, shift work, housework can take its toll on my appearance. However, recently I felt positively radiant when I happened on a WPCS qualifier and was amazed by the pristine animals being led by what can only be described as scruffy misfits. The ridden classes seemed well turned out but the in hand classes involved people wearing trainers of all things and basically whatever they had thrown in the back of the lorry cab. In fact I probably looked the part with my grey roots and fleece lined rubber clogs (my usual choice of footwear, yard to home, although I have now upgraded to leather). If it wasn't for the fact that I don't own a welshy then I may have signed up. Although I have never been comfortable with the 'death run' entrance into the arena that the welsh classes seem to have adopted.

I did used to show at county level until I discovered hunting with the bloodhounds. To be honest now the thought of bathing, trimming and chalking up to wander round a ring in hope of being picked, fills me with a feeling of exhaustion. Another parenting casualty.

Before you showing lot gasp in horror, don't forget I am a knackered mum with little filter. I do and will always appreciate a well-proportioned animal in peak condition. It's a sight to behold as we know. After all, good, correct breeding are essential in ensuring breed types remain true to their heritage. Without correct true breeding horses will be less and less able to do the job we ask of them.

Hunting

My saving grace and Darcy's saving grace I feel. Don't get me wrong, this pastime has its characters. I still question the sanity of any person who hunts, including mine. I mean who on earth volunteers to be dragged round the countryside by a half ton beast, in all weathers? Er, me!

There is an element of snobbery amongst the hunting scene; as in all of the disciplines. I am a snob myself; I cannot abide someone smoking on horseback or the latest trend of not wearing a hairnet. Here I go again....get that ponytail hazard in a hairnet before I lose all reason!

Joining a hunt can be a little intimidating but if you can find a hunt that have hunting with hounds at the heart of its concerns, then you will find they are a friendly bunch. I was lucky; I have hunted with amazing people, who to this day, have impressed me with their enthusiasm.

The hunting lot are usually a no nonsense, get on with it type of people. Not a unicorn horn or sprinkle of glitter to be seen. A horse is a horse and should be treated as so. However the odd patriotic poppy or Christmas tinsel does appear each year. One lady in particular is partial to the colour pink but the hunt are aware of her fetish and don't discriminate. In fact they built her a pink mobile jump which must look odd to some, plonked in amongst the autumn countryside.

I do remember my very first hunt. I had realised that the only time Darcy had any sparkle was while cantering around with others in the show ring. We had taken part in sponsored rides and hunter trials and he most definitely needed another horse in front to spice him up. So, as we were skipping around the ring at the New Forest Show, I was paying little attention and contemplating the idea of hunting. So little attention that I suddenly realised I had never really thought about or practiced my individual show!! That matched with my elastic band plaiting still got us qualified, so sometimes showing is not all about who you know.

One muggy day we pitched up at a farm building in the country and gave it a punt. I was not really concerned or nervous as Darcy was a true gent and the only aspect I had to keep a check on was his habit of a few bronks going into canter. In fact my hunter trial partner Simone and I had a routine. Her little pocket rocket Arab cross Poppy would belt ahead steadily and we would bring up the rear increasing in speed gradually. Once we were fully set I would shout to let her know we were ready and off we would go. We managed 4th place once.

But here I DID NOT have Simone and Poppy. So we were going to have to be grown-ups. I do remember him coping well with the sudden change in speed but was a little flummoxed by one field which was severely dotted with thistle. It must have been very interesting to watch and I can confirm it was interesting to ride, as Darcy picked his way round each thistle at full pelt gallop. Thankfully by the second similar field he must have thought it an awkward business and ploughed through every bush or plant in his way. I have never gripped so well with my knees I can tell you.

I think if Darcy had hands, he would have put pen to paper and congratulated me on my excellent decision to stop all the competition nonsense and start this hunting business. He was quite smitten.

Dressage

Undoubtedly the most difficult of all disciplines! Dressage riders are labeled the wimps of the equestrian world but believe me, riding half ton beast in a specific predetermined pattern that you have to remember in your head, is no mean feat! This takes weeks of practice, especially when you move up the grades! Dressage riders are usually perfectionists and thrive on stress and accuracy (stressage). God I'm tired even thinking about it. The downside, well, the bling. Over the years dressage riders have developed a serious need for sparkle! I mean serious crystal adorned, eye glaringly, shiny polished sparkle. Even the leather riding boots have become patent leather. Some would not look out of place in an adult catalogue. I mean really what is that all about? Oh and is has to be black, all black. Bridles, saddles, you name it. Who on earth in their right mind would chose to have horses as their hobby and then combine it with the need to show up looking like a depressed Christmas tree? Dressage riders that's who!

I have dabbled with my old horse Darcy but we could never get out of the mid 40%. Darcy had such a dislike for all things competition that I finally gave up after a very long negotiation which mainly involved him standing bolt still in the centre of any arena. Ironically bred to the eyeballs with famous competition lineage but lacked the want.

My current horse...well....very local breeding and to look at would look at home in any riding school or on cavalry parade, you know the type. However during our only second ever test came 5th with a very respectable score of 65.4. To say I was surprised is putting it mildly. I have secretly always been aware of his fabulous trot and would say he is very talented but due to our usual lack of preparation and practice I was again satisfied to just stay on. Benson was a gent whom I suppose now at the age of 8 is to be expected that he starts to mature.

As for my gear, nothing black apart from the horse and not a stitch of bling. My entire look consists of brown leather and tweed. Boots, well, baby wipes it is, usually combined with my fingernail to scrape off last season's shite and mud. In fact the first tub hunting meet is in a few days and as I write this I am very sure that at this moment my boots are sat in their boot bag, marinating in the dust or muck from whatever last outing they had.

Jumping

The pint drinkers of the horse world. A down to earth bunch who would rather give up riding than have a sparkly fake piece of glass glued on to any part of their tack. Historically very successful if you come from Yorkshire. Although some die hard millennial do try and introduced a bit of bling but they just have not come out as dressage riders yet. Show jumpers are a hungry bunch, hungry for success. Referring to the horse they are riding as 'it' rather than use the horses actual name. Not meant to sound disrespectful but may seem so when you watch them canter along, swinging their horse's head from side to side in a bid to make sure 'it' is listening. Usually prior to throwing 'it' over a ridiculously large fence. Born with balls of steel and rarely jump a horse less than 3'3 old money (figure that out for yourselves youngsters).

Eventers

Double; no triple balls of steel. My observations are that I am humbled by their choice to compete in all of the three main disciplines. I mean, who would do that to themselves?! Clearly borderline psychopaths! Not much faffing with this lot and not much bling. Occasionally matchy matchy on the cross country stage but in general a seriously devoted bunch. Downside, eventers need an army of people. So if you have one in your family, you will get roped in to helping out in some way, even the non-horsey ones will be sent off to acquire their HGV licence or be in charge of childcare and catering.

Now before becoming a parent I was into showing. My horse's choice of profession as previously mentioned. Hours of grooming, trimming, endless preening and bathing, chalking up the white bits on my coloured Darcy, until you could see him from many miles away. Now I can honestly admit that I have never fully bathed my current horse Benson in 4 years. His rump has a cluster of dust on it that will most probably remain there until the school run is no longer my responsibility.

Dressage prior to children was, practice, practice, practice. Now I watch endless tests on YouTube and give it a try on competition day.

As for jumping, I've never done a great deal, partly due to being a complete wimp and some of my horses have never been keen either. Benson my current steed is well up for it, as they say. Who knows by the time I have finished this book we may have aligned the four moons and completed a whole clear round. Our last round consisted of the only 4 jumps that I liked the look of. We did each of them twice to get my £3 worth of entry fee. My friend was running the gate that morning and I did warn her of my plan and she grinned with support as I left the ring. I do have form for this; prior to children I was disqualified at Arena UK for jumping a fence the wrong way. I kept jumping despite the bell in order to get my money's worth, much to my friend's embarrassment. For me it was a bloody great day out. I had warmed up in the same class as Pippa Funnell prior to my rebellion, so in all it was a pretty positive experience.

Eventing; well, in my dreams! I did do the odd one before kids, just a one dayer. Think that will now have to wait. Let's aim for 2027!

14

Kids and Yards

I may as well have a contagious disease now when it comes to finding livery. Add a dog into that and I now have 50% less yards available to me. I cannot blame any yard owner at all. Some liveries treat a yard as a place to ignore both children and hounds, despite them being a serious safety hazard.

We are by nature a genuine danger to any yard and if left unattended we can make for a disaster waiting to happen. Younger children waiting to pat Dobbin when Dobbin is clearly showing signs of wanting to rip said child's head off. Rowdy dogs, barking and bounding around just as you're mounting your prey animal.

Generally my children are well trained. So much so that other liveries remark on how well behaved they are, which is true. My children stay in my company the whole time. This does mean the whole task that day is doubled in time scale but at least I know all are safe which includes the other liveries and horses.

Seasonal top tip...

Summer - use the tack room as your base, cool and usually safe for the odd confinement whilst you get the horse in from the field.
Winter – favourite toy in the car, warm dry and safe, well that is unless you leave the alarm on…..that's a whole heap of trouble if you don't get that right! Spooked horses and crying kids. Glances of judgment or laughter as you claw every human and horse back down from a great height and pretend nothing happened. Juggling is a nightmare and yes my car was the car responsible!

Recently chatting with a new mum, we both admitted to choosing our stable due to its proximity to where we parked the car. Having your sleeping baby within eyeball of your quick ten minute muck out is a god send – *Maybe another TOP TIP that one!*

15

Box Rest

Yay box rest! Expensive, boring and a
nightmare to get your horse going again once it's
all over! Calmly walk you horse out for small
periods of time each day. Are you kidding me?!
This shitty task is bad enough without kids. With
kids….impossible! Fire breathing dragon and a
three year old child that you have failed to coax
into the car with their favourite toy. Just don't
even try it.

For me both periods of box rest have been after
children arrived. Easiest way is the most
expensive. Horse walker & part livery. "Straight
lines" says the vet. Cheers for that, you try
controlling half a ton that's been cooped up in his
stable for two months. I have more chance of
winning Miss World than juggling that shit. Box
rest, hate it hate it hate it! Don't overly agree with
it either but it seems to be the latest cure for all,
no matter what the ailment.
Don't mistake my disagreement with an educated
opinion, just more of an old school attitude who
has been emotionally scarred by box rest, as a
whole cruel waste of time. I have never

experienced box rest without children so I don't really express a balanced objective opinion.

I hate box rest, "yes, yes" I hear you say. No people you really DO NOT get it. I despise, hate, dread, reject, can't stand, avoid etc etc. My dislike of box rest is so strong that I have actually considered tethering my horse on one of the local roundabouts or commons in the hope that someone takes them away. My hatred of box rest overrides any reasonable rational thinking.

Let me explain……
A horse is a horse. Wild, free creatures, who we then train to allow us to ride them. Free creatures more at home in a large field than a square box. Horses are also easier to ride from the field. Relaxed stress free and less pent up energy. Muddier and hairier I admit but happier I guarantee you. Able to stretch their legs and chill. Box rest or any kind of confinement increases energy, costs money and most of all drives me nuts!!!!

I long for the old days. Ride them through it. Hack them; anything but box rest. I stare at my horse with utter annoyance, reminding myself that I am paying 5* prices to be the owner of an ornament. A large, wired, hyper, brutish ornament. Who now will not even agree, to have the bridle on without losing his shit, reacting like the bridle is made of Satan's own barbed wire, if there was such a thing. Just for that poxy 10 minutes of so called 'walk rehab', are you kidding me, ha, ha, ha, ha? (*laughs out loud in a Dracula style sarcastic tone and then immediately stops leaving a dead-pan soulless expression*).

The thought if restarting my horse again after his spell of forced box rest but undiagnosed vet result, reduces me to the weakest most negative version of myself. I am losing my mind.
My horse has now become a burden. "How harsh" I hear you say. I totally agree but box rest renders me emotionless. I even start to dislike my vet. These people who love their vet and have them on speed dial…..me, I want to send them hate mail! I do occasionally call her and convince that 24/7 grass livery and 6 weeks professional re breaking would be a more acceptable prescription but she never buys it. Re starting Benson the fire breathing dragon takes balls or desperation. I have the latter in heap loads thankfully.

I do however put on a show when the vet does visit, well a bit of a show. I pretend that I am accepting of the lack of diagnosis and the high end prescribing of the impossible.

Have I mentioned how much I hate box rest?

There, I said it. Judge me all you like, but when things go bad, juggling kids, money and a broken horse is as shit as it gets. My one weakness, my kryptonite.

My husband does not know this and please do not tell him that. This period is when I am fully open to getting rid of the nag. If only he knew. At the time of prolonged box rest if any human suggests turning away or selling or anything that cancels out this bloody slog then I would grasp their idea with eager hands. Even prepared to suggest my horse is the next Milton in a bid to bin him off. Life without a broken horse, utter bliss!

I do hope after the last paragraph you are still reading on. Please don't judge me too harshly. I have had poor results from box rest and encourage you all to plough on as your vet prescribes. (*clearly I am avoiding any possible liable suits*).

16

Livery Yards

I live on the south coast in Hampshire and in
doing so by virtue of geography; have plonked
myself in seriously poor horse country. I may as
well be in the middle of bloody London!

I have tried all types. DIY, Part, Grass. I love
grass livery the most as it is cheap and the horses
generally love it. Unfortunately for me Benson
became ill with a mystery illness and we had to
lose our space, moving to part livery for a long
spell. In fact for a horse that grew up on the
South Downs he clearly angled it so that a stable
is readily available to him and my bank account
suffers endless surprise debits.

I initially doubted whether I would add this
chapter to my book, particularly straight after my
'*box rest*' chapter, but I do feel it has relevance to
the struggle that is, owning a horse and the
additional struggle after having cherubs.

In the most part, my experience has been
interesting. Spending a fortune on livery because
you cannot support DIY horse husbandry due to
now having cherubs to bring up, only to find that

the owner who promised you the world when you were viewing the place, is on a secret mission to save every fucking penny they can!

It always amazes me when some yard owners get very precious about their grass and its survival, bleating on about poaching and keeping the horses stabled at the very faint tap of a rain drop. Yet the same owner will develop selective sight and hearing when it comes to leaky stables, broken dangerous fencing, swimming pool schools, damaged horse walkers or pot holes as big as craters in the driveway. Ironically on the occasion you do receive a rare contract it will usually state stable and grazing but will forget to mention that their grazing will be of two types.

1. Golf course standards and your horse will either remain mostly indoors.
2. Or knee high in mud due to the lack of land available.

Before kids I had my pick. I was always had the potential to be a great customer/livery. No baggage, well there was always a mutt in tow but generally they are accepted. However there was a list of what I avoided and still do today. In fact I relished those adverts which announced that children were not welcome. Well that one has come back to bite me in the arse!!!!

The definitive livery list

-*Bitchy yards*, no one needs that in their life.
-*Barbed wire*. To be honest this is me being fussy as I will accept that most yards do have it. Ideally I picture gorgeous post and rail fencing for miles, well unless you have a youngster or a cribber who will delight in chewing the shit out of it until you are either billed or given your notice (and rightly so).
-*Crazy landowners/managers.* A definite avoid! Nothing like a yard with rules that bare no relation to anything reasonable or justified. I've only ever really come across a few in my lifetime but their 'crazy' outweighed any plus points that their establishments were offering. One lady once charged me footballers rates for clearing underneath my hay pallet, referring to it a 'hay dust'. YEP that's where I kept my hay! I wouldn't have minded so much but she had on numerous occasions turned our horses out in their stable rugs leaving us with cleaning and repair bills. Knowing the difference between a stable rug and a turnout rug is pretty basic stuff. One lady also told me as I moved in that she hated taking in liveries but had to pay the bills in some

way. Ah I felt so welcome. I put this down to her having young children and may have also lost her social filter. Another lady did not like circle shapes in her sand school!! Fucking bat-shit!!

-*Vicious dogs*. No your adorable pet is not a joy to behold, particularly when he is scratching around on my car as I drive down towards my stable.

-*Poor grazing*. A pet hate for me. I mention more below.

-*Leaky stables*. It's amazing how a yard owner can become quite offended when you're hanging guttering inside your stable so dobbin does not end up wetter than he would have at 24/7 grass livery.

-*A long, hideously, unkempt track to the yard*. Only really suitable for tractors! OK, OK I am being really fussy now. We do all accept that ¼ mile before we reach our nags, we need to memorise the track down to the very last pebble in order to miss the vast crevices and pot holes. One of my yards had only about 6 metres of it but it still managed to fuck my suspension on a yearly basis!

Real plus sides would be

-*Great part livery package*. Haven't experienced one yet but I have recently been made aware of a couple of places and I intend to keep it a secret should I increase to full time work again. Most try their best but only usually for a short spell and then the bed suffers or the hay suffers or they change the package, leaving you with a lesser version of what you moved there for but for the same extortionate amount. Then they put the prices up!

-*Enough grazing*. You would imagine this as a given but believe me, many yards will try and run on a field the size of a postage stamp, resulting in you spending your life savings on bedding and hay.

-*Secure tack room*. No one likes their tack nicked.

-*Room for you horse transport that does not cost a small fortune*. One yard charged so much that I did expect the trailer to have a yearly service and monthly wash in with the price. Thankfully the chap running the place was such a financial fuckwit he regularly left this off my billing despite me highlighting that I had a trailer parked on his bosses land.

-*Facilities*. When I say facilities, a school that drains in at least two days after heavy rain and a toilet; nothing more. An indoor school is a best seller!!

-*Night time turnout in summer*. Rarer than rocking horse shit!

-Dogs on leads and children on leads. Some children are vile! I can recall many years ago, when one of my horses picked a small child up by the scruff of its jacket and promptly dropping said child back to the ground after a vigorous shake. I was mortified.

This was after a prolonged campaign headed by the child where it goaded and taunted my horse regularly (unknown to me and only disclosed after the incident).

Despite warnings from other liveries on that day, in a bid to educate the child of the damage a horse can do, the child learned the hard way. Thankfully the yard owner was the type to know horses and children and the importance of safety and good housekeeping. The parents threatened to get solicitors involved of all things but they were educated about their poor parenting skills and sent on their way.

-A yard owner who can deal with both horses and people. In the main they like the horses but we humans are a more difficult breed so I do get that we become more of a problem at times.

-Decent hacking. Good for the soul and good for the horse**.**

-Other owners who thrive on supporting each other. It does happen as I have met these people and it is a joy to behold.

For those yard owners who read the above and tick all of the positive boxes then, congratulations and carry on the good work. For you my friend are rare and pure business genius! Your dedication to both your establishment and your liveries is admirable. I have no doubt; you have a waiting list!

It's a tall order but these yards are out there, however there is usually a very long waiting list. Dead man's shoes, or dead horse's shoes should I say. I am lucky enough to have been on many a fun yard but for one reason or another (usually a house move) I have chosen to move on.

Now I know it's all personal choice and our needs do vary. We will all differ in what we are prepared to put up with. I occasionally run a problem past The Reluctant, explaining a yard issue in a bid to add some non-horsey rationale. His reaction in the most part is that of disbelief. I suppose reflecting that YES the horsey worlds compass is way off in some locations when it comes to business sense and we could probably do with some outside assistance, similar to those companies that come in and overhaul processes and departments. After all would you pay for your car to be washed but the establishment only washed the roof? Or would you pay for your nails to be done but the practitioner didn't like nail polish? -Of course not but we as owners accept a list of failings and are still willing to pay a lot of money for the privilege.

Finding a yard after children is even more difficult. Gone are the days when I could cater for my horse each day. The practicality of lost sleep and baby regimes in the early years makes it too difficult to be consistent. As children get older, parenting responsibilities alter and you main concern is their welfare. So if they are poorly or your partner is away, or you are a single parent, then packing up the entire family so you can turn dobbin out at 7am is a step too far. Well it was for me.

Before children, organising things was bad enough. Now, that social media page that modern day yards run with has updated you at 9:45 in the evening of a grand new plan involving a ban on turn out for the next number of weeks, starting tomorrow, can tip a parent over the edge. The suppressed rage that has been hidden away in a locked vault, that rage that builds up each time the livery yard adds another more difficult angle to your weekly schedule will explode and spew out in an exorcism like manner. This now involves a parent of small children juggling even more than they already do or throwing even more money at the livery yard in order to ensure the horse has enough hay, provisions and care. At least Dick Turpin had the decency to wear a mask! (*One of my Dads favourite phrases*).

In making such a decision a yard is genuinely playing with fire! We parents are living on the brink! We are all a hairs breadth away from losing our shit when buying milk! Unfortunately for me I have little filter in such circumstances and cannot stop myself 'educating' the person in charge in relation to their shoddy business skills and general crappy customer service. This in turn is never well received at any yard as customer service is not a commonly used term or practice. In fact at some yards I have been at have given the impression that I should be grateful for even the opportunity to keep my horses there. This is then supported by the meek manner in how some of the other liveries behave. Lying about why they are handing their notice in to avoid any hostility. Or not handing their notice in at all, simply putting up with the madness year after year! I think they refer to this as Stockholm Syndrome.

As I have already said, parenting does alter your goals and standards. I as a busy parent and working mum do not have the time for other people not pulling their weight. I am ticking my boxes people and livery yards should be ticking theirs in my view! I do always remember to acknowledge when an owner or manager ticks the boxes, usually marking the moment with the odd bottle of wine or small gift, after all I have plenty to say when it goes 'tits up' so to be in a position to let someone know they are a livery legend is a very nice feeling.

I may have to move to Yorkshire! I think I will have less inner hostility in Yorkshire. There is a lot of land in Yorkshire, so I hear.

I feel quite guilty when my hobby tips over to the parenting element of my life. I do recognise that this is where some of my hostility for unprofessional yards comes from. Some yards do exist in a bubble, away from the rest of the world and its advancing technology and expectation. Sitting smugly in the knowledge that we are easy money and usually desperate so will at a push go along with many a ridiculous rule or decision. More compromises to accommodate a safe environment for the occasional time I don't have childcare and want to see my horse.

On the positive side I have met some amazing people and yard owners/managers at the various yards over the years. I've met some tossers too but I think it's good to gloss over those memories.

Let's get back to the amazing people. You know the types. Always meet you with a smile and cheery chat, those that love a giggle and don't take themselves too seriously. Those who have a wealth of knowledge and only part with it at the correct time and deliver the advice with such grace that it makes you feel cared for a warm inside. Those who you would gladly help out on any occasion as they have helped you out, those who have swapped funny, amazing and educational stories and have listened to yours in return. Those who encourage and nurture, those who genuinely love to be amongst other horsey types who have the same goal, to enjoy their horse. Those characters who influence you and make you want to revisit them years later and tell them what cracking people they are and that you have never forgotten them or their wisdom. The loud ones. The quiet ones. The confident ones. The timid ones. The beginners. The experienced. The faffers. The control freaks. The show-offs. The obsessives. What a great bunch. I am genuinely fond of you all!!

There are many of you out there and I am so glad of it. You, along with my horse are what this hobby is all about. Owning a horse can be a trial and without those types of people milling about on your yard, it can be very difficult to keep focus and feel positive.

More recently I have left my yard of expensive livery and poor grazing, and have headed for the hills. Old school DIY livery again and yes I was on a waiting list. Returning to 24/7 turnout in the finer months and long glorious hacks during warm idyllic evenings. This place ticks the boxes and although it is a bit of a drive from home it means I can travel through the picturesque countryside and as I do so my soul eases a little and I look forward to saddling up and chatting with my friends. I did expect to have to compromise a little more but, yes I am allowed the children there and even ASBO is a daily visitor. Oh and get this, there is a white board where you can list things that need fixing....I shit you not!

17

Effort vs Reward

This is a short chapter which highlights that effort vs reward is slightly off centre.

After kids I am probably sat in the saddle for no more than 3 hours a week. This does increase with winter hunting but that's only due to the nature of the sport and the need to be away from home for most of the day. When you do look at the effort in relation to the reward then WTF am I doing?!

Seriously my friends, bills, mud etc, I've said it all before. The problem is, that whenever I feel like this, mostly at the end of winter time, it all melts away when I walk up to Benson and see that he is waiting, ears pricked, expectant with a little flicker in his nose, greeting me in his usual thuggish manner. How does he do it (smiles). Not forgetting the good days, crisp winter days with a clear sky, hacking around quintessentially English country villages, chatting to your horsey friend and putting the world to rights, or the foot perfect competition resulting in a ribbon or a decent score.

Make no mistake the effort is far greater commitment than the short lived reward but somehow we accept it, allowing ourselves to put the negative stuff aside and enjoy the moment.

18

Confession.

Things I have done…..

1. Put my sleeping child in the next stable (empty) like baby Jesus, while I tend to my horse.
2. Fed my awake child excessive snacks in order to keep him from wanting to leave the pushchair.
3. Make my child sit on the stored jumps (with food) while I lunge the beast.
4. Transported my children round in a shitty, pissy wheelbarrow so I can get stuff done. They love it btw and will ask for more!!
5. Locked my children in the car at winter turning out or bring in time. Gale force wind is never a helper! Safest place for them but from the outside looks a bit harsh.
6. Purchased mini persons mucking out tools and barrow to encourage the idea that being locked in a stable with me is a fun idea.

7. Convinced my children that blistering cold and torrential rain is just the kind of fresh air they need.
8. Sledged my firstborn 1.4 miles in deep snow when the whole country was at a standstill. Clearly not child cruelty as he bloody loved it and was in a snowsuit so very cosy. Although the sledge seemed very light at one point, thankfully it did not take long for me to notice that my one year old had rolled off. Again not cruel as he thought that was hilarious!
9. Ran out of snacks so provided my children with carrots from the manky feed bin. It never got as far as pony nuts but I bet you parents are out there!
10. Considered hooking my sons walking reins to the outside of the stable, however the physics of it all meant that there would have been a lot of natural force in a semicircular direction which even by my standards wasn't in the good parenting book. Let's all just take a minute though and accept that such things can be necessary consideration!

19

Clothing

Prior to children I would not think twice about spending a week's wages on an item of clothing or equipment that promised to turn me into Mary King or at least look a bit like I know what I'm doing.

Well, now you're lucky if I have washed my t-shirt and jodhpurs in the last month. Such items are usually thrown back under the stair cupboard as soon as I walk into the house. This is after an ungodly 05:30 military operation start to sneak out of the sleeping family home to grab a few minutes in the saddle. In fact most of my clothing is pre baby, 15 year old jods and t shirts living their last breath. The bonus side to having children is that my measly 3 hours a week in the saddle means little further wear and tear.

TOP TIP - The one warning I would give, when with child, store your gear well!
I didn't and underestimating the amount of time out of the saddle. I left my gear muddy, unclean and dumped. Zip by zip and button by button my clothing has gone into shock with the renewed use. Slowly disintegrating after each short use, reminding me that my now new feeble bank

account will not push to another fine pair of leather chaps or a new style body protector. Try replacing that lot on part time wages. DEPRESSING!!

I have been quite frugal in how I have resolved such dilapidation. My chaps were in general ok but the elastic had withered slightly and a lady had borrowed them, a lady with bigger calves than me (*this is not an easy achievement*) leaving the poor elastic stretched beyond their maximum and had never returned to normal size. I toddled off to the local saddler and had them repaired, along with my hunting field boots as they, although not stretched, the zips had slowly given up the ghost during the last hunt, leaving me with an interesting look and not at all waterproof.

Oh and can anyone tell me why body warmers (*gillets to those who like to be a bit posh*) all have an obligatory hole inside each pocket within 6 months. I have lost count of the times I have to route round through the hole and round to my back to find my car keys. Not sure this is a consequence of parenting as I think it happened prior to my cherubs.

Now the school run is here I have mastered the art of the outfit change. Some days housework outfit, school run outfit and yard outfit are all needed. All placed in the dining room ready for me to burst into the house get a quick change (picturing myself in catwalk mode or Wonder Woman style spin) and on to the next scheduled part of the day. Any visitor to our home will undoubtedly view my school run bra hanging proudly (or slightly greyish and withered), waiting its turn.

Housework outfit is usually some serious slouchy clothes, not even fit for the tip. The yard outfit, usually varied clothing ranging from very expensive purchased from the local tack shop to cheap as chips, bought from a foreign food outlet along with a drill and garden shears.

Finally the school run outfit. A masterpiece of false advertising, usually a Jules sweatshirt twinned with a country coat, printed scarf, jeggings and chic classic style boots.

All of which can be topped off with a hat to hide either, horse riding, sweaty hat hair or morning school run hair, unsure of which is the less attractive. Genius move! To display to all that twice a day you are a MOTHERING LEGEND. Occasionally marred by my panicked morning walk due to the battle I have in getting two little cherubs out of the fucking house before half 8. A very good friend of mine firmly believes that a suitable hat and fabulous sunglasses are a must for the school run. *Quote "The hat hides the hair that has yet to see a brush this morning and the sun glasses mask the lack of available time to put make-up on"*

It even fools my husband when we have the rare '*both parents picking up*' event. He always compliments me on my appearance and then the façade is taken off as soon as we get home, replaced with my housework clothes, his reality showing in his expression as I whip off my 'look' and replace it with a dowdy version of myself. You see readers; I told you I was a fraud.

20

Rosettes

I won my first rosette at the age of 11 and my first red ribbon at the age of 19. The red one was courtesy of Apollo Silver Stream, a gent of a horse, who I had on loan for a short while. This loan arrangement was after admitting defeat with a youngster who I had bought and then sold on (another story).

The level of pride and joy as it was handed to me brought tears to my eyes. It was a very small local show but the achievement was reflected by my beaming smile. Over the years I have collected many cups and rosettes, qualifying for a national show being my most obvious achievement. I never did go to the national show as although my lorry was fit for purpose, it would never have made it so far up north. I also knew that my horse at the time was stunning but lacked the confirmation and I lacked the fame to be placed in the line-up. I was however, so proud that we had managed to qualify.

Since children the first rosette I was awarded, was out of pity. Benson being the brut that he is, decided to overachieve at the hunt sponsored ride.

By overachieve I mean thrash his owner (me) to within an inch of selling him!

Unable to comprehend the idea that a sponsored fun ride was a system of groups of riders, having a gentle bimble around the countryside, Benson's goal was to catch up to the next group in front. And then the next group and so on and so on.

So in a bid to avoid being binned and watch my horse finish the many mile ride in a full flat 10 minutes, leaving carnage in his wake, I hatched a plan!

I would walk next to him, to alleviate his anxiety and mine. You know what I mean, that horse whisperer moment where my steed locks on to my powerful caring vibes and throws his trust and wellbeing into my hands. Dispelling any bad thoughts and tension he may have had, instead walking calmly beside me knowing that I will guide him all the way. We become as one!

Suffice to say that it was a bloody long two hours resulting in a shit load of blisters, sweating in a body protector while I composed, in my head, a suitable for sale ad (again) with Benson in mind. During this time Benson waited for any slim opportunity to fuck off! So yes I gained a rosette out of pity. One of the hunt members openly felt sorry for me and thrust it my way with a beaming smile on her face. I was in full agreement with

her, I was deserving of this endeavor. Mostly for not going home with an empty trailer!
On reflection having children fogs my rational thought. I had just trained my horse to hunt and Benson does air on the side of keen and I recall I was feeding him from a bag (remember the country chap?).
My nerve was gone and little time in the saddle had made me desperate!

We have gained rosettes since and each one is a 'power pack' of positive for me. Improving and realising small goals is how I keep going. To have a nice little ribbon to hook up in my truck on the way home as Benson stands quiet in the trailer confirms to me that the journey is going in the right direction.

21

The Horse.

Well some of you will have been lucky enough to have the same horse before, during and after childbirth. I was not as I have already mentioned. Although now I will admit that despite the hideous experience of losing Darcy, I am not one for turning the clock back or wishing that some life experiences did not occur.

The only time I feel a slight pang for my old horse is usually when Benson is causing me a complete cluster fuck of a day! Although even in his later years, hacking Darcy on his own was no picnic. So me even trying add a rose tinted, gentle hack around the block memory (*back in the day*) to Darcy's CV is bull!

Historically with Benson the cluster fuck has involved clipping, loading, tacking up, jumping, farrier, you name it, he will have some type of extreme aversion to the events unfolding in front of him.
This has resulted in him either pissing off somewhere or if enclosed, belting the shit out of whatever has him confined, standing on me,

ditching me, wrecking my tack or any other nearby equipment.

When you have a 'made' horse it is a real adjustment to then return to bringing on a youngster, even more so when you're a new parent with little time to make mistakes or fix them after the horse has bolted.

One glorious Sunday morning of child free time, in an effort to bond and get Benson back on the road to fitness, I thought naively that long lining in the local forest would be an excellent opportunity for us to gel.

Boy how wrong was I?!

My first mistake was to take the dog. I pictured an idyllic walk with the pooch trotting alongside in harmony with me and the steed as we moved through the beautiful Autumnal surroundings. Instead the ASBO fucked off in to the woods only to reappear at various stages to check I was still going in the same direction. This in turn gave Benson the task of freezing on the spot each time ASBO came hurtling towards us.

Secondly the forest sounds so lush doesn't it, yes, however it is also full of dog walkers with ASBO dogs such as mine, who on hearing and seeing the excitement of my pooch and a large black giant dog like animal (horse), also lost their shit and in

the case of one Bull Terrier, decided to hang off
the back of my horse's tail in some kind of death
wish maneuver.

On this particular occasion ASBO, Bull Terrier
and my horse all disappeared into the distance
with my flailing lunge lines trailing behind. The
Bull Terrier, which was brilliant white in colour
against the pure blackness of Benson's tail,
moved further and further away as ASBO
returned to my side in an almost insulting show
of obedience. I wanted to flip her the bird but
was far too busy.

Oh and there was a slightly shocked and worried
owner amongst all this who may have been quite
surprised by my calm reaction to events, however
I will never know as he too disappeared and I
never saw him again. I will assume he retrieved
his dog as thankfully when I found my horse the
mutt was not attached.

I initially jogged back in the direction of the loose
horse, which by now I had no doubt, had trashed
several general members of the public in his path.
My jog slowed to a paced walk as by this time I
was done! I do have a habit of replacing pure
rage or panic with deep calm and sudden extreme
decision making. Well why not, how the hell was
I going to throttle the other dog owner, catch a
cantering horse and save every member of the
public from injury, all on my own?! Impossible!

So you calm down and accept your current fate as it unfolds.

Done with horses, done with dogs and in fact all things shitty and rural!

The only consolation was that I remembered I had public liability insurance which although not ideal, may dig me out of whatever disaster was waiting for me.

I continued for about a mile, passing families with push chairs and groups of normal people on bikes, all enjoying what appears to be a pretty fucking chilled day until literally a few moments ago.

Some of them pointing open mouthed in the direction of my horse's trail of destruction.

Lastly meeting a lovely member of the public who was not at all horsey, with lunge line in hand and a lump of a horse puffing and sweating but walking along behind. She was quite taken with him as most people are with Benson. I thanked her repeatedly and took hold of him only to find that in all of this I had dropped one of my new gloves along the track somewhere.

So there I was, defeated, cheesed off, at the end of my tether, looking for a brand new brown leather glove in a very wooded and brown environment. I pondered for a while about how I would have felt if I found the glove and had never found my horse again. For a split second the glove alone seemed so appealing!!

I did however take a small positive and surmised that he had clearly had a good bit of exercise so it may be a good idea to get back on him tomorrow. SILVER LININGS!!

I did try this experience for a second time without the dog but it was ruined by a couple of unruly Husky types who again seemed to see my horse as a giant prey animal rather than the half tone of flesh that could render them extinct with one swipe of his hoof. Poor Benson. In his defense he never once kicked out at any of these dogs so I suppose I should feel grateful that his answer to the problem was to just go back the way he came. I cannot describe to you how deflating this period in our relationship was and in all honesty it was neither of our faults, just circumstances. He had been quite poorly and I had nearly lost him. I was skint and sad due to having to move from 247 grazing (easy life) to part livery and an unprofessional one at that. I had spent some time building him up and starting him off again so to have something like that happen twice was a real blow.

My reaction was to let the dust settle and to allow a bit of reflection and move on. So you see I have a real ongoing determination to have a 'made' horse again. This was a few years ago now and we have improved despite both me and Benson being what can only be described as shit magnets.

We have never ventured back to the forest!

Oh and don't be mistaken, there have been utter disasters prior to children and Benson. Incidents that I cringe at even the thought, however time did not seem so precious and desperate back then so the failures not so poignant and soon forgotten. Well that and being in my 20's and 30's and not having the life thrashed out of me through lack of sleep and the request for a school fundraising homemade fancy dress outfit with 2 days notice!

22

Injuries

Yes injuries. Any injury is never fun. Falling off, being stood on, bitten, kicked, dragged to name but a few, are all most inconvenient and bloody painful when they do occur.

Prior to my little cherubs arriving, injuries were never welcome however; now, they must be avoided at all costs, particularly as my undercarriage regularly reminds me that I have pushed out two children and it will not tolerate any more tom foolery.

For I am now the centre of the universe. Headquarters. The main woman. The prime minister. Master of all I scrub and clean. The one and only person who knows where everything is, even the shitty plastic finger toy with the glittery wings, lost at least three months ago but has now become the most singularly important item in her toy filled bedroom.

The only one who can put the washing machine on or feed the chickens without stepping in dog shit that the ASBO has left on the lawn. The only one who can use the toilet brush when it is required (my husband has tried but no one likes to see anyone reaching and gagging to the point of no return). Which reminds me of a story…..

Picture this, a frantic mum getting ready for an early shift on New Year's Eve, juggling waking, sleepy, hungry children and a husband trying to have some sort of lie-in upstairs. In walks ASBO from the garden. Crouches her arse down on the kitchen rug and proceeds to deploy a 2 feet long skid mark on said rug. So in amongst all of the above I now have ten minutes to literally 'sort this shit out'. Mmmm I pondered; could The Reluctant deal with this like an adult? Leaving me to whisk myself off to work and be a professional for the day.

I know; I will test the water. I called The Reluctant to come and assist me quickly and explained what the subject matter was. He appeared in the room a very short time later and immediately gagged so badly that I thought he may bring something up. He repeated this gag three times and even with his t-shirt over his nose, he failed the test and I was now back to my 10 minutes of time to finish getting ready, wash a dogs arse and shampoo a carpet.

I maybe should have known better as from past experiences The Reluctant does not do anyone else's poo. Once while quite pregnant he offered to do my share of the poo picking. Not the best job, even when you like horses. He managed a whole wheelbarrow to then turn and state that that was one of the most unpleasant tasks he had ever had to endure.

Yes it's just me, just me who runs this house so that we can go to work, eat, get to school on time and all in clean clothes and with full lunchboxes. Please don't mistake my above sentences for arrogance. My husband could no doubt do all of the above but I've not the nerve to let him.

The other day I asked him to take a sack of chicken pellets down to the bottom of the garden as my back was a little twingy. He did just that, no more and no less. It did not occur to him to take off the feed bin lid and store the sack away, instead the paper sack was left in the drizzling rain to get soggy and spoil. In the end I went down and stored it away only to return to a puzzled look on my husband's face, as if to suggest that I was being fussy.

So you see I am the Queen of all that I clean and care for so NO - injuries should be avoided at all cost.

Now that is not to say it does not happen. I have been ditched by Benson a few times and each time received an injury ranging from a wrenched thumb to mild concussion. The pressure increased greatly by The Reluctants usual grimace and snarly comments when I do come home with a limp or bruise. I do recall a pre kids fall from a horse many years ago when my parents came to pick me up after I had fallen off jumping. My back had gone and could not drive. They dropped me off at home in the care of The Reluctant who promptly fucked off to play golf, leaving me order food on line.

Ironically one of the more recent mishaps was running through mud in wellies due to some horses being turned out and aiming straight for me. I initially felt such pain in my calf that I thought I had been kicked, turned out that I had torn the muscle from the ligament. I limped back to the yard and nursed myself home. Thankfully the lack of being on a horse made the delivery of my story much more palatable for The Reluctant. I was on crutches for a good week but continued with my responsibilities, well I did stop riding. Oh and the horse went lame shortly after so for the next 6 weeks my life was shit!

23

Loaners.

I have tried the odd loaner over the years but I find myself drifting from being quite a relaxed owner to an owner who then realises that I may not be that relaxed.

Benson can be a challenge too and as honest as I am about him I still hold my nerve when someone tries him out.

In the main I want someone to ride the horse on the couple of days a week that they have him. Not groom or faff or dote, someone who will get on his back without fail so that I can add their riding time to my horse fitness calendar in my head. Initially I thought that the fault was with the loaners but now I do accept that my relaxed manner encourages loaners to not pay, not ride, not even turn up. Leaving me with the cost or responsibility for ensuring the horse is mucked out etc. on that day. Again I know I sound a bit brutal but again motherhood is a busy, unforgiving business and last minute cancellations or tack that cannot be sat in due to fuck off lumps of clay mud from the loaners hack the day before adds pressure to what is already a busy week.

So now it's just me. Evenings of schooling or hacking after the kids have gone to bed. In fact when they were babies I regularly rode at half 5 in the morning before the world woke up, albeit for a short 20 minutes but it was time in the saddle so job done. Oh and make no mistake I was bloody knackered to the point of insanity but shit had to get done.

I have also learnt that when someone else rides your horse there will always be telltale signs of rider's different habits and ways of going. I do sometimes let Benson go hunting with a lovely capable young chap. Benson had a ball and it was very interesting to school him a couple of days after. Total lack of concentration and treated each corner of the school as a platform to anticipate a great launch, as if he was imagining entering a large stubble field braced for the first stride of gallop. If any of you know that feeling, it's good shit but makes for a wobbly schooling session and certainly does not get you a streamlined change of rein. However, I have been very relaxed about this as its part of my plan for him. Learning he has varied jobs is essential for the type of horse I want to produce. Nothing

Badminton level, just a good all-rounder with a bit of sparkle (no rearing Benson, just sparkle!).

24

Utopia

Well today it happened. It actually happened. I rode my horse while my two children sat in the gallery watching. To any non-horsey parent this may sound pretty beige. For me and some of you out there it sounds nigh on miraculous. Two children, one 9 and the other 4 sitting quietly without arguing, needing a poo or wee. No falling off anything, no sudden sounds which would result in me getting binned.

Unfortunately it kind of happened by accident so I doubt the situation will ever repeat itself, especially if I try and orchestrate it again, that would just be stupid. The four moons would not be that kind to me surely.

I was about to leave the house and have a bit of me time so popped upstairs to give my sleepy family a kiss good bye when both children suddenly claimed that to come with me to the yard in the dark, would be fun.

My heart skipped a beat, not because I had a moment of 'mummy love' knowing that my children wanted to be with me but because my precious mummy horsey time was about to be utterly ruined by two children who will no doubt push me to my limit while I muck out, fill buckets and stuff haynet's! Why did I just not bolt out of the house when I had the chance?!

Oh and riding, shit I wanted to ride. My selfish half hour of equine connection was now seriously in jeopardy. However I did the calculations and knowing that the previous afternoon Benson and I had had a lesson, an hour long one, at which point we were both blowing out of our arses and dripping with sweat. I surmised that if the children could be quiet for at least ten minutes, Benson would be knackered enough and mature enough now to keep his shit together for the ten minutes it takes to reaffirm what we had learned in the lesson the previous day.

Fuck it, we can do this! (There's that FUCK IT thing again). If they can land men on the moon then I can ride in the company of my offspring. Hardcore horsey parenting time! In any case, a bit of fresh air and helping your mum with the horse can make for two tired children ready for an afternoon movie at home while mummy has a cuppa and writes her book, bliss!

Well I tried and I pulled it off!!

We even finished the morning walking the ASBO cockapoo in the fields while my two adorable children recited a well know children's book about hunting a bear, while sploshing about in their wellies. WT actual F!

It was like the front cover of one of my magazines, you know the ones that depict an idyllic life walking along wearing a trendy short tweed skirt, flowing blouse with flawless skin and salon perfect hair. All against a beautiful country backdrop with my imaginary country mansion nestled in the background of my 50 acres. No dark glasses or hat needed here, just blissful country life.

As if that wasn't enough, when we arrived home (Victorian town house a slight come down from my imaginary country mansion) my gorgeous husband had some bacon on the go in the pan, having taken full advantage of his surprise free time and been for a run in his new trainers I had bought him for Christmas. He too was experiencing utopia. Selling the perfect morning to our children as quality family time, while disguising what we had really done (our hobbies).

I mean if that's not an advert for the perfect active family morning then what is?

Parenting utopia!

25

The End

My little girl started school in Sept 2018. With both of the cherubs at school and my working shift pattern allowing me two whole days to myself a week, I am now giving it some horsey hammer! Not going to lie, I am embracing it. I have already trailered out to a few friends' yards for a hacking catch up coffee morning (you cannot beat that shit).

Children do not stay babies for long and life does move on. I loved my days alone with both of my little ones. A chance to make memories and just hang out together, ensuring one day a week was totally horse free. No planning around turning out or bringing in. I have to say it was lovely not constantly clock watching, although as we all know my livery bill reflected the cost of this wholesome plan.

Some days we did not even get into the car, just walking into town, buying sweets and going swimming. My daughter's transition to school has filled me with emotion as did my sons pending start at school years earlier. I'm so glad I made time for the both of them as the years are flying by and I can always look back at my early time with them and know that we were best buddies.

I close this chapter of my book fully indulging in my own thoughts and words, knowing that I wouldn't change it.

I adore my children and I love horses. Could I do with winning the lottery? Yes. Could I have made a more considered approach to choosing my career and lifestyle? Yes. How easy would my life be with my own land and a job that I could complete from home? An absolute breeze! However I don't and am not waiting on the lottery to realise my vision.

Instead I will plough on as most of us do. Juggling and grasping at the windows of horsey perfection while those four moons align. The one constant that I do have is that I worship my children and all that they bring. My husband although not rural, is my best friend and between us 'we got this'. I bloody love my life. It's busy and exciting and I am adored, what's not to like?!

Good luck to you **all** out there, whatever horsey path you are on x

Printed in Great Britain
by Amazon

58614441R00080